THE D MENTALITY BOOK

A GUIDE THROUGH THE INS AND OUTS OF DATING AND RELATIONSHIPS

CHRIS FINLEY

CONTENTS

PREFACE

This book was inspired by encountering and spending time with men who were close friends or colleagues of mine. They were socially awkward and depressed, many of whom wanted to be in a relationship or get married and start a family but they were unsure of how to approach and meet women. Being the type of guy I was, able to walk the line between being both an athletic, self-assured guy and what they referred to as "a kind of nerd", they could relate to me.

My studies in sociology as an honors student and playing sports in college allowed me to interact with intellectual introverts and athletes. I now feel obligated to share my knowledge, understanding, and conclusion about relationships and dating. Hopefully, a lot of what I put in this book will help a lot of guys know they can find love and a relationship with the woman they desire.

Since I started college, I've had 15 years of experience being in relationships, which I've used to write this book. My six-year first marriage and subsequent relationships with women, whether dating or in a committed relationship, have all come and gone. I've gone through failed relationships and gained an understanding of my mistakes through reading about women's behavior in books. There were a lot of times when I would go through a difficult situation with a woman I was seeing. I would write what she said and how I reacted to whatever situation it was, and if my responses worked to maintain her attraction I would note that down. If they didn't work I would put it down as a mistake to avoid in the future.

This book about dating and relationships is special because I not only verified what I read in books about specific meetings with women, but I also compared my analysis with guys who have had success dating women, and with close friends of mine who have been in committed relationships.

**There's two things that you're gonna find out. They don't love you, and they only love you right now. If I was smarter, I'da stayed my ass at home

And leave them Broadway girls alone**

LIL DURK FEAT. MORGAN WALLEN

INTRODUCTION

When I was a young man, it was challenging for me to go through life's changes and develop into the man I wanted to be. Trying to learn on my own how to be masculine and meet women. As I was growing up, I wanted to meet and interact with women without getting nervous or struggling to make conversation. Although I was one of the many students at my school, I was shy and only attracted girls' attention because I was a smart student and a member of the Spelling Bee team. I did little socializing when it came to the opposite sex.

The only reason I tried to get good grades was so that I could help the prettiest girl in class with her homework. When I talked to a girl, it was usually one of the unpopular geeky girls who were on the chess team or in the drama club. Those that the other guys had no interest in or wanted to be seen with. This was the closest I had ever gotten to a girl at the time. And most of them happened to be in my honors classes.

Some of the guys I've met over the years have asked me the same question at some point: "How do you pick up girls?" They observed me approaching girls, dating, and getting to know other ladies while I was out and about. Often, I wasn't even dating or acquainted with the girls they saw me with. They just assumed that I was. However, how I impulsively approached girls always fascinated them. These guys couldn't seem to get that just because I spoke to a woman I had never spoken to before, it didn't mean I was attempting to gain her phone number or ask her out on a date. They thought that every time they saw a man and woman interacting in some way, they were in some kind of relationship, either married or just dating. They didn't get that sometimes men and women just chat.

I wondered why most guys felt this way, and I concluded that they didn't interact with many people of the opposite sex in their daily lives. I noticed how they kept quiet when a girl they didn't know passed by and instead just gave her a sideways glance. These were the kinds of guys most would refer to as "squares" in high school.

In this book, I'm going to give you the benefit of my experiences involving women. I'll tell you what I've discovered about dating the kind of woman you've desired and what it's like being in a relationship with an attractive woman. Also, how you can maneuver difficult situations in terms of interacting, dating, dealing with a woman's mood swings, rejections, and dating on apps. I hope this book serves as a guide for you while you find the woman you've been looking for.

CHAPTER 1

APPROACHING THE WOMAN OF YOUR DREAMS

EVER SINCE I was a young man, I've wanted the prettiest girl in school. But I quickly realized my extreme shyness, especially with approaching an attractive girl. I remember when I tried to speak to a pretty girl I liked, I would freeze up while trying to say the simplest word, "Hi!"

Once, there was this pretty girl at my school who I liked. She always spoke to me whenever she came around, but I could never respond to her fast enough before she walked away. I usually became lost for words and over thought about what my response should be. I ended up looking like a weirdo for looking at her too long when I was trying to think of something cool to say back to her. When I had the chance to talk with her, I blew it horribly.

It was the last day of my senior year in high school and her locker was next to mine. She was alone, getting stuff out of her locker, and I was doing the same. This time, I was determined to speak to her. It was do-or-die time. This was on the last day of school, and I tried to ask her what she was doing now that she had graduated. When I tried speaking to her, my voice quivered, and I mumbled something incomprehensible.

So I raised my voice and repeated myself a little louder, or so I thought. She looked up at me and then asked me if I had said anything. I responded with a quick "no." She grabbed her things out of her locker and walked away. I never saw her again after that. I was so embarrassed and disappointed in myself for not being able to speak loud enough so she could hear me.

That situation haunted me for a long time. It's bad when you're a teenager and you never forget the girl you had a crush on. It's even worse when you're an adult and remember the first and last name of the girl you had tried to talk to when you were in high school, but failed. After that event, I committed myself to never again let a girl I'm interested in make me so nervous to the point where I couldn't communicate with her.

Soon after, I began reading books about women's behavior to better understand how I interacted with them and where I fell short. I quickly learned how to approach and converse with a girl without being timid or nervous. Sometimes, I would occasionally push myself to approach attractive women outside of my comfort zone. I made a point of talking to a woman I wouldn't normally expect to approach in public, even if it was only to say "Hi." Doing this enhanced my self-assurance and increased my comfort with being around attractive women.

When you ask women you are attracted to out, you need to be bold and assertive when you approach them. Be direct about what you want and your intentions. Don't beat around the bush, talking about things you don't care about and why you approached her in the first place. And don't waste your time with useless conversations that don't benefit your goals. Most men do not realize that there is nothing more attractive to women than a man who approaches her and knows what he wants. It shows her he has a high sexual market value and that he has options.

This means that when you approach her and she first notices you, although she may be in a relationship with someone else or otherwise unable to date you, she will still find you attractive. She will think you are the only man she can still get to know. She will appreciate the fact that you approached her and expressed interest in her because this shows you are the kind of man who goes after what he wants, which is extremely alluring to women. Asking a woman out is the only way to get her attention and show her you are interested in her. It's astonishing how women seek these traits in a man just by being direct and assertive. As visual beings, men are more interested in a woman's appearance and beauty, such as whether she has a pretty face or a nice body, for example.

Women appreciate attractive men and men who have decent looks, but they also pay close attention to a man's level of selfassurance, boldness, and assertiveness. They truly value that in a man. You don't have to be particularly attractive to catch a woman's eye, but you also don't want to come across as timid.

OVERCOMING SHYNESS
The only reason I came across as a little more outgoing and sociable is that I grew up in a neighborhood where it was important to be aware of your surroundings. I can remember that every summer when I was younger, I was sent to live with my grandparents out in the country. They made sure I spoke

to everyone politely and spoke up so they could hear what I had to say. My grandfather would tell me, "Speak up, boy! Has the cat got your tongue?" if I spoke too softly. Considering that, I was taught to speak when I first met someone new, regardless of who they were. This, I believe, played a role in my early confidence and character development.

Many young men go through their whole high school and college years, never approaching a girl or never talking to the type of girl they want. They're usually too shy to approach them. According to Dictionary.com, shyness is defined as the state of being reserved or having or showing nervousness or timidity in the company of other people. Shyness is an emotion a lot of men struggle with through their younger years.

But this emotion, which is the feeling of being uncomfortable, is something most young men should try to conquer before entering the world of adulthood. These young men must be able to maintain a masculine frame around any type of woman they come across.

THE MASCULINE FRAME
What is your masculine frame? Well, it isn't your build or physique, although this does play a part in it. It is the method of interpretation you use to figure out a certain event or situation. It comes from having a healthy balance of the mind, spirit, and body.

According to HeroRise founder Isaac Cotec, the masculine frame is the embodiment and projection of a person's masculinity. It is a combination of masculine energy, emotional control, and self-confidence. (Cotec, n.d.)

Cotec goes on to say, *"A masculine frame comes from being mentally, spiritually, and physically balanced." "It's about being confident without being dominant, stoic without being callous, ambitious without being ruthless, and competitive without being psychopathic."* A man with a masculine frame walks with assurance, assumes leadership roles, and can sometimes be viewed as a role model for others. (Cotec, n.d.)

If you have a masculine frame, you come across as confident, assured, and assertive. Handling a woman's conflicts will set you apart from other guys if you can handle her in return. This will allow her to want to give herself to you.

Developing a masculine frame is how a man creates a powerful aura and how he carries himself. It's not about how you walk down the street with your chest up, but how you handle sticky situations, as a man should. Unfortunately, most men today lack a masculine frame.

It's important to understand here that a masculine frame is not a biological thing. Females can take on a masculine frame when they have those traits referred to above. Nor has it anything to do with sexual orientation. Having a masculine frame does not make a woman a lesbian in the same way a man with a feminine frame is not necessarily gay. It simply means they have taken on different roles.

Over the last few years, there has been a massive decline in strong male role models for men to look up to, both in their personal lives and in the media. A study in the UK has shown a downward trend in the perception of masculinity among young men (18 to 24-year-olds), with only 2% considering themselves completely masculine. (YouGov, 2016)

A male father makes an enormous difference in a young man's life. He can teach him how to handle situations, how to carry himself, and how to take on challenges that emerge unexpectedly. Even having uncles around can teach younger men how to be men as they grow up. The Institute for Family Studies estimates that about 70% of men are raised by their biological fathers, so 30% are not. These men lack the upbringing to become masculine and have no idea how a man should act. A boy who does not have a male role model to help guide him through life is at a tremendous disadvantage compared to other men who have strong fathers or male role models.

A boy who only has a mother or a father with a feminine frame is more likely to develop the feminine characteristics of those people around him rather than the male. However, some guys see the result of their upbringing and reject the feminine side, despite not having a father or father figure to take them under their wing and show them how to take charge of their lives and be more masculine.

But even then, boys will frequently take after an uncle, a cousin, a brother, or even a TV character like James Bond. Despite the lack of male role models in their lives, many of these men have grown into the most powerful men in society.

So, if you didn't have a male role model when you were growing up, what can you do to develop your masculine frame? It is not just a case of acting more "manly." This might not come naturally to some men who have been raised in a predominantly female environment, and it is important not to push it because this can lead to other issues (which I will deal with later).

Therefore, the first thing you must do is learn about yourself. Understand why you feel less masculine than your imaginary role model. Is it about looks or physique? You don't have to be the best-looking guy or have a six-pack like Schwarzenegger to attract the kind of girl you dream about. All you need is confidence and an aura that says, "I'm a man, and I'm proud of it." If the woman you're going for is looking for a man she can rely on to take care of her when necessary, you have to show her you are that man. (Cotec, Holding a Masculine Frame)

Once you know your level of masculinity, the next step is to focus on your interactions with others. This involves actively listening to people, showing empathy, and communicating effectively.

This naturally leads to developing emotional awareness. Recognize your emotions and let them out naturally rather than holding them in. The key to being a masculine man is showing others that you have feelings yet are strong enough to handle them while helping others manage their emotional issues. Women like to know they can rely on a man for emotional support, not someone who will collapse at the first sign of a problem. (Cotec, Holding a Masculine Frame)

I mentioned before about the problems that can arise when acting against your natural tendencies. I'm trying to show you how to develop your masculine frame, not become a monster. If you think being masculine is about putting on a show of strength, being the tough guy, acting aggressively, and not showing your feelings, you're wrong. This is what is known as "hegemonic masculinity," where men end up suppressing a whole range of emotions, needs, and opportunities, including the pleasure of caring for others, receptiveness, empathy, and sympathy, which are felt to be inconsistent with masculinity. (Kaufman, 1999)

The aim is to attract the woman of your dreams. Now that you've developed your masculine frame, let's move on to the approach.

THE APPROACH

Asking a woman about her day, cracking a joke to make her laugh, to ease the tension of nervousness before asking for her phone number, is a good way to start a conversation. What I mean by this is that you should introduce yourself to a woman you don't know before striking up a conversation by asking her where she is from or asking for directions. It's simple to bring up a joke once the conversation is underway. This worked for me once: "Hey, have you heard why alligators don't like clowns?" "Because they taste funny." OK, I'm sure you can do better than that, but if you can't, maybe stick with the directions. Then move on to her number.

So, before making that initial approach, you need to identify your target.

I have frequently heard men say they are looking for a particular kind of lady, but they are never willing to put in the effort to find the type of woman they want. However, some men claim to seek a specific type of woman but end up settling for the one they already have, despite their claims. I constantly wonder how they will handle women who they think are of a higher caliber than the ones they are used to dating when they can't even handle the current ones.

I have experienced this desire myself and realized that if I'm not able to approach or handle the emotions of the women I'm with, how the heck am I going to handle a Gal Gadot or a Zoe Saldana type of woman? If you're a big DC/Marvel movie fan, you'd know who I'm referring to. The movie star type of woman is what most men have always been drawn to as the ideal woman they would like to date. A lot of men go through life hoping they can be with this or that type of woman when they can't even handle the one they're with. My question to you? How are you going to handle actress Gal Gadot's (who starred in the movie Wonder Woman) emotional bombs when she shit-tests you?

What I have noticed with some guys is that the type of woman they prefer isn't as attractive as the woman they're with. There is a reason for this. What you have to realize is that the more attractive a woman is, the bigger the emotional shit-test she's going to throw at you. It's her way of weeding out the weak link among potential suitors and seeing if you're the type of man she can trust and who will take control.

The best thing you can do to win a woman over and make her want you is to pass her "shit test" by not collapsing at the first hint of her getting angry or agitated. You may wonder how. Realize that her feelings are temporary, and don't take her irrational behavior or disapproval of whatever you said or did personally. Demonstrate to her you are the type of man you claim to be by choosing not to argue with her. By doing this, you can surely have the girl you want if you can manage these situations.

Getting back to the subject, how do you approach the woman you have had your eyes on for the past week or so?

Well, first, do a little research. If she's worthy of your attention and you are keen enough to make that first nerve-wracking move, you should at least try to find out what sorts of things she likes. Is she into music, and if so, what bands does she like? What about sports? If she enjoys baseball, purchasing a few tickets for the upcoming game is a good way to start a conversation…

Some advocate buying flowers, but in my experience, this is a dangerous move if she is not your girlfriend or wife. It can make her feel uncomfortable when you buy flowers or gifts for a woman you don't know. Then there is the aspect of timing. There is no point in pushing a bunch of lilies into her hands when she's on her way to meet friends. Besides, if she's never even noticed you before, it may come off as creepy—she may think you've been stalking her.

That leads me on to the next point. If the lady hasn't indicated that she is aware of your presence, you're starting from a low point to begin with. You want her to think that you are someone worth spending her valuable time with, even if it's just for one date, so get yourself noticed in the best way possible.

Use your masculine frame to your advantage. As I said earlier, looks and physique aren't everything. Beautiful women attract handsome men, but that doesn't mean these hunks are better than you in any way. If you've mastered your masculine frame, you are already at an advantage because they probably don't even know what that is.

If you're in a bar, try to catch her eye. Give her that smile you've been practicing, then look away, share a joke with someone, and laugh. This gives the impression you like her, but she's not the only one you're interested in. Always look back, though. You don't want to be too cool about it.

Plan what you're going to say and practice it. When you do make that first approach, you don't want to fumble your lines like I did when I was first starting out in this game.

Check her mood. There is no point in asking her out if she is obviously upset or angry. Getting her on her own is sometimes the easier way to approach her, but if you're brave enough to approach her while she's with a friend, it shows her you're not afraid to go after what you want as a man.

Remember, you can't assume that because she's attractive, she's probably got a string of men lined up. That doesn't imply that you're wasting your time if you ask someone out on a date. Don't give up if she turns you down on your first date; all that means is that she might have weekend plans. Think ahead and decide what you want to do in the coming week if she does say yes.

Ask her directly for her phone number. Tell her you think she's attractive, and you'd love to get to know her better, letting her know you will call her. If she gives you her number, you know she's interested, but don't wait too long before calling. I once had the embarrassing situation of having to describe myself and tell the lady where we met because she'd had a lot of guys hit on her in the meantime.

If she says no, don't take it personally. It may be just the wrong time or the wrong place. Be nice about it. There may be someone else, or she may just not be interested in you; who cares? Move on. There are plenty more out there.

In the next chapter, I will let you in on some secrets I learned from my experiences with first dates. I know how nerve-racking this can be and how easy it is to make a total ass of yourself. Get it wrong, and there will be no second date. Get it right, and you could be heading toward a fun relationship that you can work on.

CHAPTER 2

YOUR FIRST DATE AND BEYOND

ONCE YOU HAVE SECURED a date with the woman you have targeted, remember that first impressions count. OK, you got past the first hurdle of asking her out, but that's only the beginning. Now you've got to concentrate on your first date. Once you've been doing this for a while, this part will come as second nature, but for someone new to the dating game, it is important to get this right.

First, think about your appearance. What to wear, how to style your hair, clean shaven or with stubble beard? Here's a tip. Don't waste too much time thinking about how to impress her. Think only about what makes you feel good. Don't enter into a relationship as someone else—you'll struggle to keep that up for long.

Second, don't be too casual. It's one thing to dress to suit yourself, but you want to show you have made some effort. Keep in mind your masculine frame and dress in a way that reflects that. Tight-fitting shirts look great on a slim guy, but if you're carrying a little extra weight, wear something less figure-hugging.

If you have thought this through properly, you will have arranged to meet her on neutral ground. The last place you want to be is at your neighborhood bar, where your friends might show up and join in on the fun. Furthermore, for the same reason, you don't want to meet her in her neighborhood. Choose a venue close by where neither of you is well known whether you decide to pick her up or arrange to meet her somewhere.

This brings up the third point, which is, what kind of venue do you frequent? This largely depends on your date. If she enjoys fine dining, then a fancy restaurant might be the best option. But this has its drawbacks: affordability and too much, too soon. You want to keep your first date simple and easygoing. Consider what you can do to ensure that you both have a fun time on your date.

Trying to impress a girl by going somewhere really pricey can backfire on you if you are embarrassed when you get the bill. Even if you agree to split the cost, you don't want her to feel bad if she can't meet her side of the bill.

Also, be sure to know what you're eating. If you try to impress by ordering escargot, don't balk when a plate of snails arrives.

Certain types of food aren't great for a first date. Garlic can put a girl off if she doesn't like the smell, and spaghetti can get really messy if you don't know how to eat it right.

My advice is to stick with what you know and find out beforehand what she would prefer. You wouldn't want to take a vegan to the steakhouse now, would you? Find someplace that's quiet enough for you to hold a conversation, but not lacking in atmosphere.

Sports venues can be fun if you know she's a baseball fan, for example. They are a good way of relaxing and not having to drive the conversation. Beware of rivalries, though. If you're a Yankees fan and she loves the Red Sox, you might be better off sticking to bowling.

According to a survey by the dating site Match, the number one thing that women want from their first date is to feel comfortable. Nearly all the women surveyed said they liked to be complimented as well, so remember this when you first meet up. (Dodson, 2018)

Other tips:

- Don't drink too much. Any more than two alcoholic drinks might be considered heavy on the first date.
- Arrive early, certainly before your date does.
- Keep the conversation inclusive. Don't just talk about yourself all the time. Ask questions, but don't interrogate. If you have been conversing before meeting up, raise some of the things she mentioned about herself. This shows you've been paying attention.
- Avoid taking her to the movies. It's impossible to have any conversation there. That can come later when you've become more acquainted. Making out on the back row is a thing of the past!
- Don't be rude to the waiter. This is a turnoff for many women. In fact, be generous with the tip.
- Be confident. Women like someone who takes control. Be spontaneous. Show her your adventurous, fun side.

Regarding physical contact, the Match survey said that 82% of women like to be hugged and 71% expect a kiss on the cheek. They also thought it was important to be a good kisser, so pucker up those lips. As for sex, 83% wanted a man who was enthusiastic about it, but good communication was essential. Be open and show you care about her views on sex. It might not happen that night, but play your cards right, and maybe next time.

THE NEXT STAGE
Assuming that went well, you can ease yourself into the relationship, and subsequent dates won't be so bad.

I really blew my first attempt at dating a beautiful woman. I kept my cool for the first three weeks of dating her, during which I acted as if nothing moved me by maintaining a masculine frame when I was around her. Not until she started telling me how she felt about me did I realize it. She talked about how I differed from most guys she'd dealt with and how I made her feel comfortable. With her confessions on how she felt and saw me as a potential future boyfriend, I became overconfident and quickly eased into being too nice, or what some would call a "beta male" mentality.

I started putting her needs before my own. This was because I was too inexperienced in dealing with this type of woman. She noticed I was slipping into being Mr. Nice Guy too soon. One weekend, when she came over to my place to hang out, we lay in bed kissing and cuddling. During a moment of passion, I confessed how I felt about her and the 'L' word slipped out. I told her, "I love you, and I hope you don't leave me." Man! I feel so stupid just writing this. I cringe at the thought of it.

After I said those words to her, the whole vibe of the room changed, along with the look on her face, as if she were disappointed by my confession. After a while, she looked at her cell phone and came up with some reason, saying she had to return home. She kissed me goodbye, and I never saw her again after that. A few days later, I tried to contact her, but neither my text messages nor phone calls ever got a response.

When it came down to the woman I was genuinely interested in, I could not keep her because I could not stay in my center to show I was stable enough to be with her. Even though I was dating other women, I showed my cards too soon in the relationship, mostly because of my impatience. I was thinking to myself that I needed to close the deal so as not to lose her to someone else. Even though I had only known this girl for a few weeks, I was still a beta male when it came down to it.

I lacked the Alpha Male Mentality that would have made her follow me. Instead, it led to her losing interest in me and her respect for the type of man I was supposed to be while I was with her. When you meet the type of woman you are interested in and who you regard as extremely attractive, you will subsequently come to understand this.

You shouldn't be concerned if a woman leaves you. You shouldn't be too invested in her, you should have other priorities, or you should value something else over her. More than ever, you'll need to meet other women. even if it's just to chat or hang out. It's not necessary to have sex with multiple women, but if you date more than one woman, you'll keep yourself from concentrating on just one.

Always keep a woman second in your life, especially at the beginning of a relationship. Have a woman by your side at all times, even if it's just someone to talk to, but don't make that woman your priority. Whatever your interests are, focus on your career and work on yourself and your hobbies. When a man has an insatiable passion for achieving his goals, he becomes much more desirable to the women he wants. A woman should only be a complement to a man, never the focus of his life.

GIVE EACH OTHER SPACE

Don't spend so much time with a woman because you believe she will think you don't care if you don't. In reality, being away makes her more curious, and makes her wonder what she's missing out on, or what you do when you're not with her.

For example, if you haven't noticed the recent increase in divorce following the pandemic, marriages and relationships where two people shared a home have ended. This resulted from spending too much time together. Making the woman too well acquainted with the man.

In the early stages of a relationship, when the intensity and passion are at their peak, it can be relatively simple to maintain a girl's attraction. You must first continue to elude her to keep her intrigued. She doesn't have to be aware of every detail of your life just because you are starting a new relationship or are in a committed one. She doesn't have to be aware of what you do, where you go, and what you're working on.

You still need to catch her off guard. It's crucial to have the ability to surprise your partner. This does not, however, entail bringing flowers or other gifts. It entails being unexpected in your personality, attitude, and actions. Spontaneity is a great attraction for most women. You must do things she doesn't expect. By doing your own thing, your own projects, and having your own ambitions, like working out whatever it is, you need to do things like this for yourself. This is very good for the relationship, especially in the beginning.

What most men don't realize when they are in a relationship is that it's okay to be selfish and all about yourself. That's why I think so many men are miserable when they are in a relationship and are lost when it's over. They don't put themselves first. You don't want to be too close to your partner all the time, even if you're in a long-term relationship. People get into the habit of being close. That's why you want to pull away a little. This will surprise them by not always being available all the time and not responding to their messages right away.

Don't fall into a routine where you have to see each other every day, or every Wednesday, Friday, or Sunday. Mix it up, change things around, and be surprising. This will keep her on her toes and make you much more interesting as a man. To help with this, you must understand the basic principles of attraction: similarity, proximity, reciprocity, and anxiety. (Exploring Your Mind, 2020)

PRINCIPLES OF ATTRACTION
Harry (H.T.) Reis is a professor of psychology at the University of Rochester, and he has done a lot of work on interpersonal relationships, addressing stuff like gender and sex, dating, partner responsiveness, principles of familiarity,

and perceptions of similarity. So, this guy knows what he's talking about. Here are his four principles of attraction.

1. The Principle of Similarity

While familiarity can promote attraction, it can also do the opposite. The more you get to know someone, the more you can discover traits that you either like or dislike, and this boils down to similarity and dissimilarity. It seems we like people who are similar to ourselves. (Reis et al. 2011).

While it may be true that opposites attract, it seems women are more attracted to men who share the same interests and concerns as they do. There are three reasons for this:

1. Validation of what they are and think, which brings them satisfaction.
2. Reaffirmation of their interests and tastes. They must be good if others share them.
3. Sharing their environment with others without conflicts or sacrifices. If you both like dancing, you dance.

(Exploring Your Mind, 2020)

2. The Principle of Proximity

According to Reis, we are more likely to form a relationship with someone close to us. Living or working in the same neighborhood provides more opportunities for interaction, even on a casual basis initially.

If you see a beautiful woman who frequents the same coffee shop as you, you're going to have at least two things in common —coffee and sharing the same environment. The chances are you have mutual friends or similar concerns about local issues.

But one word of warning. If you wait too long before making a move, the principle of proximity states that the attraction can become unfavorable. Ever heard the saying "familiarity breeds contempt"? The antidote to this is curiosity (Lambert Couples Therapy, 2022). Always maintain a state of active interest until it's time for you to approach the lady.

3. The Principle of Reciprocity

A man is likely to be more willing to approach a woman who he thinks will respond favorably toward his advances. This gives us a feeling of confidence and stimulates positive thoughts about ourselves.

Reis stated that the principle of reciprocity overrides the principle of similarity, so we are more likely to be attracted to someone who accepts us as we are, despite having little in common.

4. The Principle of Stress and Anxiety

This principle states that we seek the company of others when we feel frightened or threatened. This makes us feel safe and helps us form a bond with the person we seek.

Converting this into a dating opportunity, be the proverbial "knight in shining armor" when the chance presents itself.

Let's say the lady you're attracted to is accosted by someone in the street. Maybe they try to steal her purse, and you just happen to be close by, so you step in and save the day.

I know this may sound far-fetched and highly unlikely, but the principle can be applied to far less threatening situations. For instance, you're in the shopping mall and you notice she is struggling with her bag of shopping, so you go over and offer assistance. Hey, it's the adult version of carrying her books to school.

To sum up, knowing the principles of attraction might not help you get that first date, but it will help you understand how our minds work and will improve your chances of success.

In the next chapter, we will look at the dating process itself, and what to expect during those early days of a relationship.

CHAPTER 3

DATING

So, now you're dating. Well, you've gotten past the initial process of going out for a drink or a meal, and you're in a good place. You have her number, so you can stay in contact, but you're only going to call her to set up a date, not to have a chat about your day. You never want to have long conversations on the phone. It kills the attraction, and you end up giving her too much information about yourself.

If you talk too much on the phone, some women will use this to find out everything about you and decide they don't need to go out with you. You're not a mystery to them anymore, and they no longer want to get to know more about you.

So once you have set the time, date, and venue, that's it. Kill the chat. This may be a good time for tried and trusted movies and a drink afterward. It gives you the chance to get used to being around her, especially if you don't have a lot of experience dating women.

After the first date, leave a 3-day window before you call her again. This gives her time to call you if she enjoyed the date, and doesn't make you sound desperate if she doesn't.

When you're out on a date with her, you want to be there to have a good time. The first thing on your mind shouldn't be sex. Just have fun. The more a woman enjoys herself being around you, the more she is willing to go home with you. Usually, on the second date, you should ask her to come over to your place to hang out. Such as, "Would you like to come to my place and finish this conversation?" When the mood is right, you will know.

By now, she should be comfortable enough to be alone with you. Here's something I learned about women when they decide to come over to your place. She expects you to make some kind of move on her. As a man, she is expecting you to at least try. This lets her know you're the type of guy who will go for what he wants.

Women are turned on by this because it shows masculinity. If you don't at least try for sex, I promise you, you will never see her again. Women like the idea that you want them. But if you have the chance to advance and don't take it, she will see it as you being too nice and will not want to date you again. Then be prepared for her to put you in the friend zone.

If the second date doesn't lead to sex, it's okay. By you at least making an effort, it lets her know what type of man you are. If she's willing to go out with you on a third date, she definitely still has an interest in you.

When asking her out for a third date, it should be the same process as date number one and two. Keep your conversations on the phone or in texts short and to the point. But this time you're going to ask her to come over to your place. This is your chance to set the mood. You can either cook for her or order out. Either way, your third date should be at your place.

If she comes over to your place, she is definitely interested in having sex with you. You have got to make sure you are doing everything right in order to keep your interaction romantic. If she doesn't want to be intimate, don't get upset.

Just end the date and don't call her again because you don't want to waste your time. Move on to someone else who has more of an interest in you. You have to assume that if it had been a different guy who was significantly more assertive with women than you, she would have had sex with him most likely on the first date, but most definitely on the second.

Here is some advice though: if you are around other men who are eager to socialize with and meet women, you will be too. If you hang out with guys who constantly approach women, for example, you'll approach girls yourself. If the guys you hang out with merely sit around playing video games and watching movies without trying to talk to women or pick up chicks, you'll probably act in the same way.

Men have worked together since the dawn of time. This is how guys navigate through life to try to continue to survive, whether it is through fraternities, sports teams, or the military. In order to succeed in approaching the ladies, find a crew that is interested in ladies and not just beer and football.

PUTTING HER ON A PEDESTAL

Putting women on a pedestal has one big drawback. To win over a woman he finds attractive, a guy will do a lot of things for her. Offer to buy her drinks and take her on a fancy date. Some guys go so far as to buy her gifts or take her on vacation during their initial dating phase. Most men act in this way because they hold women in high regard but, due to their appearance, they don't have the confidence to rely on their charisma alone.

Guys who do these things to impress a woman don't realize this does not work in the real world. And women don't think like that either. There are two significant reasons why. First off, pursuing a woman—for sex, dating, or a relationship—makes you inherently a follower because the person who exerts more effort to make something happen sends a subliminal message to the unconscious mind that the woman has something she has to offer that you want. If she believes she has worth and that you are after her for that worth, she will hold back as much as she can because you are telling her that she is the prize.

And secondly, understand that a woman has to choose you, meaning that there's nothing you can do or say that will make a woman like you. So even if a woman meets you, gets a sense of who you are, and feels chemistry after getting to know you, she might still not like you. Remember the Principle of Proximity and maintain a level of curiosity. There isn't much you can say or do to influence how she feels mentally and emotionally about wanting to be with you.

In addition, you cannot buy a woman's approval, which is what you were attempting to do when you gave her gifts. And this is a common mistake made by men who believe that if they meet a woman and try to impress her by smoothly talking to her, they will be successful, such as by telling her what they can do for her, what kind of man he is, what his career is like, and how successful he is.

That will neither impress the woman nor grab her interest in wanting to be with him. What you have to understand is that attraction is an emotion, not a choice. Therefore, sex and relationships must develop naturally and through chemistry when two people are dating. You cannot force a woman to act or feel attracted to you in the manner that you desire.

BE YOURSELF

The best dating advice I can give you is to be as genuine as you can be and dress to the best of your ability in your own sense of style. And when you speak with her, bring up topics that interest you. The woman should perceive you as getting to know her, letting her know who you are, and being comfortable enough to step back and listen to her when she speaks.

This is the Principle of Similarity at play. If you don't state what you believe in, how can you ever find out if you have similar thoughts and interests? I've known some guys who always seem to look for approval.

Seeking approval can become an addiction in some men who don't have confidence in their own beliefs. The trouble is, men like this have rarely expressed their views in public for fear of upsetting or annoying their peer group. My advice is this. Start by practicing in the privacy of your own home. State your view on something out loud and think about how it sounds. Is it so outrageous?

Don't let the need to win people over force you to put their preferences ahead of your own. Doing this can lead to thought patterns that go against who you truly are. (Exploring Your Mind, 2016)

Social media, and Facebook in particular, has become a minefield of keyboard warriors who simply want their voices to be heard or to shoot down the opinions of those who disagree with them. Don't become one of them. Speak out if you feel strongly about something.

If you have to convince a woman that you are her best option by jumping through hoops, proving yourself to her, buying her stuff, and telling her what she wants to hear, she's not the one for you. Because it is obvious that she does not view you as her best option, she may believe that you are merely one of the many male orbiters who are waiting to be with her, or she may think that you are ok and that a better option may present itself, in which case she will move on to be with someone else.

Let's imagine that after doing all of these things for your woman, you manage to persuade her to move in with you. The power dynamics of that relationship will be in her favor, which is what will ultimately happen. resulting in you committing to a life of ensuring she is happy and making an extra effort to win her favor.

Unfortunately, this has been the model in western society, which is why a lot of women dislike hearing it from men. They believe it's a man's responsibility to appease a woman, ensure her happiness, take care of her, and so on. Actually, it is the complete opposite.

You have to learn to say no to a woman, as well. Lots of guys I meet tell me how they feel oppressed, under the thumb of their partners. Guys I've known for a long time lose their identities, change their opinions to match their girlfriend's, and even stop seeing their friends. They are scared they might lose her if they stand up and speak out against them. Then they wonder why the girl left them for another man. Her parting words were, "It's not you, it's me."

Women are very good at shaping their men to think as they do. They will express an opinion and then say, "Don't you agree?" The easiest course of action is to say yes. The hardest thing is to say no, but often that is the best way to go. A woman will respect a man who has firm beliefs. They may think they like to shape their man, but in reality, they want someone who has a mind of their own.

One guy once said to me, "I gave her everything she ever wanted, took her everywhere she wanted to go, and then she ran off with my best friend."

"Well," I told him, "you should have said 'no' more often." He gave her everything he thought she wanted, but the truth is, she wanted a man to lead and give her the things he wanted to give her. Like sexy lingerie. Telling her how good she would look wearing it is a real turn-on for them, despite what they might say.

AVOID SLIPPING INTO AN ABUSIVE RELATIONSHIP

When we talk about abusive relationships, we usually think about women being abused by men, but I've seen many men suffering from abuse by their long-term partners.

Abuse doesn't have to be physical to be harmful. Mental abuse is far more common and less likely to be noticed. We can see cuts and bruises, but we can't see inside the mind. And women are very good at getting into your head.

Mental abuse often takes the form of gaslighting. You must have heard of this. It's the number one word of 2022, according to the Merriam-Webster dictionary, which defines gaslighting as:

> "The act or practice of grossly misleading someone, especially for one's own advantage."

I have come across this on many occasions. Gaslighting often causes the victim to doubt themselves and usually comes out during an argument. The woman will say something like,

"I'm sorry if you think I hurt you." While this statement might seem like an apology, it isn't. She has deflected responsibility for hurting your feelings onto you.

This kind of apology leaves you questioning your own judgment and wondering if you did overreact.

If you accuse your partner of lying about something, she may say something like, "Do you really think I would make that up?" They are attempting to make you feel guilty for not trusting them. When you hear this, you doubt whether she is actually lying, questioning your own understanding of the truth.

(Ladderer, 2022)

Always be on the lookout for giveaway phrases that make you doubt yourself or your sanity. It's a slippery slope.

In the next chapter, I will delve into the mind of the Alpha Male and show you how to become less Beta and more Alpha.

CHAPTER 4

KILL THE BETA MALE IN YOU

A BETA MALE is a man who lacks masculine energy. He is an introvert, sensitive, a bit nerdy, and was likely bullied at school. A beta male is often taken advantage of because of his "nice guy" persona. Women tend to like beta males more as friends rather than lovers.

When I was young, I remember trying hard to be a nice guy in school. I was hoping to be the type of guy girls wanted to talk to and who saw me as different from other guys. When a girl told me I was such a nice guy, whether it was because I opened the door or helped her carry something heavy, I wore her words like a badge of honor and felt proud. I had hoped that since a girl saw me this way, it would result in her wanting to be interested in me, and I was a better pick than the other guys she was dating.

At least that's what I thought from watching all the TV shows and movies. The problem with these shows and movies is that they usually show the nice guy as the hero who gets the girl at the end. As long as he keeps doing all the right things to show the girl, he's different from the other guys, he will end up with her and live happily ever after. That is what I believed growing up. I thought I would have this happy ending of being with a girl who saw me for my kindness.

Beta males watch all these rom-com movies and TV shows and cannot understand why they fail miserably with women. They don't see that the guy on TV is just a persona. He isn't real, and, in reality, things don't work out that way.

Your persona is the face that you show to the world when you're trying to pretend and convince yourself and others that you are harmless and a good person.

But a good person isn't always harmless. A good person is capable of anything, and they can be the worst kind of man to be around. They attempt to be perceived as nice people but bottle everything up inside. Then they try to hide who they are and what they desire from the world. I would prefer to be in the company of a man who, while still being himself, I know to be dangerous. At least I can rely on his character.

The Bible states in Psalms 37:11 that "but the meek shall inherit the earth, and they shall delight themselves in the abundance of peace." This provides some justification for why humility was regarded as a virtue in biblical times. When left in peace and undisturbed, the meek cohabit in harmony. People who are capable of force but decide not to use it are in the proper moral position.

"What he meant by that was that most of what people claim to be a moral virtue is merely their fear of doing anything that they would actually like to do, that society would deem inappropriate, has nothing to do with morality whatsoever."
— Jordan Peterson

Most cowards pass themselves off as nice people. They pretend to be a person who is safe to be around, yet in actuality, they are a danger to be around because they are frightened to be who they truly are. They think that being nice shows their goodness. It's a façade that men put on to seem

32

like good people to both themselves and those around them, so they can picture themselves as decent people who do nothing wrong when they look in the mirror.

You can get out of the beta male thought pattern in several ways. Examining your resentment can help you face the reality of who you are in this process. That may result from a variety of circumstances, such as not getting what you want. When you don't get what you want, you must realize your frustration.

You can tell by the way a man enters a room and interacts with others in a social setting if he is well-developed and has some grace. It's because he has allowed both his compassionate and aggressive sides to shine through.

Essentially, when you are in that beta male mindset, especially with women, pay attention to your resentment of being assertive and what it is trying to tell you. For instance, you might walk her to her car after a first date. Your inner beta is telling you to be kind and avoid being confrontational. You don't want to annoy her or give her the impression that you're creepy.

In circumstances like this, pay attention to this voice. Do the opposite if you hear this voice. Attempt the kiss or hug her. You don't have to ask; it's okay. Women like a man who asserts himself. She will let you know if she is not interested in your advances. If that happens, back off and realize she might not be ready for an intimate relationship with you.

Another move is when you're sitting down and conversing with her after the date and you're at a loss for words. Kiss her and surprise her. Show her you know how to be a leader. Spontaneity is good in a man,

After repeatedly having unsuccessful relationships with the women I preferred, I realized something wasn't right. I then realized that I had to kill the beta male within me. I know this sounds harsh, but if I wanted to grow as a man and become the kind of man who can achieve his goals in life, I needed to be aware of how I act and work to live a more manly life.

To emphasize what they might consider my alpha qualities and to get past the beta male mindset, I had to adopt an "I don't care" attitude to accomplish this. I developed the habit of not caring what other people thought of me. In my younger years, I took it very seriously. I used to worry about what other people thought of me. That someone, especially a girl I liked, felt I was a bad person, probably made me anxious. Having an "I don't give a fuck" attitude is the key to being a man. I think a man needs to separate the bullshit from what matters to him and use it to his advantage to succeed in life by killing the beta in him so he can develop into something greater.

Killing the beta male within you does not imply that you will take on the role of the alpha male. It simply means that you exhibit more alpha characteristics. Alphas are extroverts. They are natural leaders who dominate in any group situation. This is not something any ordinary guy can just decide to be. However, by being confident in your masculine frame, you will become much more attractive to the women you are hoping to date.

In the next chapter, I will tell you how to overcome the fear of being alone. I will show you how being needy will lead to the certain death of a relationship and why you must lead the relationship to keep it alive.

CHAPTER 5

BEING NEEDY

WHY ARE you needy in relationships? For most men, it comes from the fear that they will never find someone to be with. Fortunately enough for me, I could date multiple women, even though they weren't what I wanted. I had never been without a relationship for long periods because of my insecurity about being needed. I thought that being married would guarantee a relationship with a woman who would stay with me. I believed that if we got married, she would be obligated to stay with me forever.

It took two failed marriages for me to understand I was sadly mistaken. From those experiences, I quickly realized that I was not terrified of just being alone; rather, I was afraid of being rejected and alone. I yearned to experience desire from a person of the opposite sex. What is needy?

"Needy" is a term used to characterize a host of behaviors associated with an acute need for physical or emotional attention. According to the Good Therapy Blog (GoodTherapy.com), PsychPedia's article simply titled "Needy," neediness is an excessive need for acceptance or affection that results in that person repeatedly becoming overly attached to people and depending on them too much. (Johnson, 2008)

Insecure attachment is often the culprit behind clinginess in relationships, according to relationship expert Jaime

Bronstein, of the California Licensed Clinical Social Worker (LCSW). "It occurs because the person fears they will be abandoned in some way or unloved, and it most often stems from childhood and their relationship (or lack of relationship) with one or both parents. In addition, an insecure attachment style can develop from previous romantic relationships if the person feels like they weren't prioritized or didn't receive enough attention or love from their significant other," she says. (Lloyd, 2022)

You ought to ask yourself, "Why am I needy?" Is it because you want to be married and in a committed relationship? You get comfort from the belief that someone cares about you. A successful relationship cannot withstand this kind of insecurity. This explains your fear of being abandoned if you experience it in your relationship. The fear that the woman in your life may leave you and never come back.

Another possibility is that you may fear losing a woman's affection. Do you feel secure in a woman's affection? Do you feel you can let your guard down? It's really difficult to repair your walls after they've been destroyed. There is no such thing as letting your guard down entirely around a woman. The ability to lead a relationship as a man is something you need to develop. To do this without losing your girlfriend or wife, you'll need to have good emotional management skills. It will help you regain your composure. A woman needs a man who leads and loves her, not one who follows. If she doesn't respect you as a man, then any attempt at romance or seduction will only fail.

To keep the relationship going, you must be the head of the household and take the initiative. Working on activities you find enjoyable while focusing on oneself is one way to do this.

Now and again, skip a few days without seeing her. There is time for you to discover and develop your masculinity. You need to become a better version of yourself, and the man you've always wanted to be, whether you're spending time with the boys or traveling. You must do this, especially if you want to maintain your attraction to the woman you want to date. In addition, don't be preoccupied with your relationship. It's not a good idea to focus just on one woman. Also, refrain from giving in to your insecurities because doing so will damage your relationship with her.

> *"Here's a side note to remember when dealing with attractive women. The more feminine a woman feels around you, the more comfortable she feels around a man she likes. "Be the man, and learn how to manage your emotions properly."*

> BRUCE BRYANS, 2013

In his book, *What Women Want In A Man,* Bruce Bryans wrote, "...in *every* way, in order to attract and, more importantly, *keep* a good woman in your life, you must become the kind of man that she simply can't live without. This is your only job as a man when it comes to dating and relating to women."

The truth of the matter is that romantic relationships are a part of life that some of us will experience at some point in our lives. What many people don't get or understand is that when they get attached to someone, they mistake their longing for neediness. We've been told time and time again that being needy is a sign of weakness, a lesson we've learned since we were young children.

What you should aspire for is self-reliance—getting to the root of who you are and what makes you do the things you do, so you can understand yourself and other people much better. Here are some things I've learned about attachment needs, relationships, and what research has to say about neediness.

ATTACHMENT THEORY AND DATING

According to many sociologists, attachment is a biological necessity, not a bad thing. Your brain is wired to seek and form attachments. Researchers in sociology, relationship science, and physiology have repeatedly shown the validity of this research.

In actuality, most people are only as needy as their unfulfilled needs. Attachment is defined as a "lasting psychological connectedness between human beings." (Bowlby, 1997)

In the 1940s and 1950s, when parents were urged not to over-cuddle their children, the notion that individuals were overly dependent on others became increasingly prevalent. People believed that with your children, you should strive for separation and distance. They thought children would become overly dependent, but when those needs were not addressed, children did not grow up to be well-rounded adults.

In addition, your brain has a pre-programming mechanism known as the attachment system. Attachment theory was the seminal work of John Bowlby (1958). In the 1930s, Bowlby worked as a psychiatrist in a Child Guidance Clinic in London, where he treated many children who needed emotional support. According to Bowlby, attachment can be understood within an evolutionary context because the caregiver offers the baby security and safety. Attachment is adaptive, as it enhances the infant's chance of survival. In order to survive, children are biologically predisposed to form attachments with others when they are young. (McLeod, S. A. 2017)

This attachment system shows how our brains are constantly monitoring and seeking out our parents' or other people's help in meeting our needs. That could be interpreted as physical or physiological.

For instance, if you leave a baby alone in a strange environment, its brain is pre-programmed to seek out the mother and satisfy those attachment needs. Adults experience the same situation. This is where the sense of what we perceive as neediness appears. It makes no difference where you are in the relationship or how long you have been dating. Your brain is wired to operate in this way.

This explains why you occasionally feel anxious and agitated over a relationship that's not fulfilling your needs. We must acknowledge our reliance on biological realities. It is like how you must breathe oxygen, eat food, and drink water.

What would you want to do to exert some control over this behavior? And what can you do to alter your perspective and consider whether this person is the best fit to meet your emotional requirements, as well as whether they can and will do so? What most of us have been taught to do is to consider "would they like me?" and "am I good enough?"

Work on developing a better understanding of your own needs for things like coaching, reflection, and journaling so that you can convey those needs to your partner and ensure that their needs are met as well. If you don't, you'll be stuck in a cycle of responding mindlessly to the unmet wants of your attachment systems. Many people have told me they mistakenly think they are this needy person when, in reality, it's only their attachment system that isn't fully developed. In particular, males have been taught to suppress these emotional needs, and society views them as weak men when it is a biological fact in the natural world.

The pressure society has placed on many males in today's world to not act needy around women might perplex many guys, but it's better to show emotion than bottle it up. It's how you deal with that emotion that matters. A woman will like you for handling your emotions well. She will know she can trust you with hers.

Be powerful without coming across as needy to foster a positive connection. Neediness is not about expressing emotions, and it only becomes problematic if it is abused. Let's be clear: neediness results from a deficiency, and neediness requires validation. Confidence does not cause neediness. Here are a few instances of how interacting with women has different needs.

First, there is a distinction between saying to a woman, "I like you and I'm into you. I think you're beautiful, so let's get something going," and ending there.

Second, a man might say, "I like you, and I'm into you." He then approaches her the following day and declares, "Hey, I'm really into you, and I like you a lot," after which she receives a text that expresses his interest in her and his liking for her. So he asks, "What are we going to do about it? I want to be with you." This is neediness. The overdue request is to be validated by her.

One of the biggest pieces of advice I can give you to detect whether you are needy or if you're just showing feelings is to always come from an abundance mindset. By having an abundance mindset, I mean having the confidence that there are other women out there you might date, that you have choices and that she isn't the only one you're now seeing.

Try to get rid of the notion that she is the only woman you will ever be with. That is a scarcity mindset. And please don't feel obligated to tell her how you feel early in the relationship to keep her. Outside of abundance, say to yourself, "I know what I want, and I'm going to focus my wants and limits on establishing the framework for communicating that to this woman."

I'll leave you with this last thought regarding neediness. Always remember that the woman you're dating should do the same in return. It doesn't mean you show her your feelings right away and open up to her if she doesn't reciprocate when you're with her. You continue to maintain your boundaries. You should imitate her behavior instead. For instance, don't be the only one in the relationship who puts everything on the line to get what they want; instead, exhibit your emotions as much as the other person does. Neediness occurs when you place a higher priority on what others think of you than what you think of yourself.

"The root of all unattractiveness is neediness; the root of all attractiveness is non-neediness."

MARK MASON

So guys, here is the number one thing you must do if you want to get out of being needy. And the only thing you have to do to get all the girls you've ever wanted is this. While you go through your daily life, try to drill non-neediness into your head.

Here is an example of neediness versus non-neediness. A needy person wants their friends to think they're cool, funny, or smart and will constantly try to impress them with their coolness, humor, or smart opinions about everything. A non-needy person just enjoys spending time with their friends for the sake of spending time with them and doesn't feel the need to perform around them.

In other words, after talking to her, you truly don't care whether you get a girl or not. You can't fake it, even if the girl you tried to pick up was super attractive and everything you ever wanted in a woman, and she ends up not talking to you or ghosting you. Be in the mindset that it doesn't matter. I'm just going to move on to the next girl to talk to.

You have to not let it affect you, and once you can truly download non-neediness to your brain and think from a non neediness paradigm, you've got it. People around you will sense this from you, and positive things will happen in your life. Because of a peculiar law of the universe, we tend to push away the good things we need and want most. Thus, those things enter your life when you genuinely don't need them.

You can get that mindset by understanding two things. One, some people are just not right for each other. Sometimes a relationship just doesn't work out. What they provide and what you need don't match, and vice versa. It is just not a good fit, so you move on.

Number two, which a lot of guys don't understand, is this. Many girls have a certain type of guy they are interested in. So if you keep shooting your shot with a certain girl and she keeps turning you down, move on until you find the girl who thinks you are her type.

In the next chapter, I will show you how to deal with mood swings. Good luck with that!

CHAPTER 6

SHE'S MOODY

WHEN I FIRST STARTED DATING AND getting into relationships, I didn't know there was a certain ability you needed to have as a man when dating to deal with a woman's shifting emotions, particularly if the woman you're seeing suddenly displays moodiness out of the blue. In the beginning, I would always lose my cool and argue with whomever I was dating. When I argued with a woman, I didn't know I was fighting a losing battle. I lost countless relationships because of my inexperience in dealing with women and conflict.

I would constantly allow a woman to knock me off my pedestal and force me out of my masculine frame into a weak state of mind where she could push my button easily. It wasn't until I got older and went through more heartbreak that I understood I was confirming a woman's feelings. Whatever emotional issues she was experiencing were not my concern, nor should I have attempted to fix her. All you can do at this point as a man is to be there for her and be supportive.

What happens when a lady suddenly turns nasty and criticizes everything you say or do is something I was unaware of at the time. But what I found out through my series of dates with many women is that, in the first place, she is pondering her feelings for you and whether you are the kind of man who can handle her emotions. She is challenging you to decide if she wants to continue with you or not. By doing so, she'll be able to tell if you're the right guy.

A lot of times, what she does isn't on purpose; it's subconscious. For some women, it's hard to tell you she needs some space, or that she wants to see someone else without making you feel bad. But then she will suddenly distance herself from you, causing havoc or making excuses for why she hasn't been able to spend time with you. And sometimes it might not even be something you did, or it might just be a test of your masculinity.

My advice when you notice this type of behavior is to let her know you need time apart or enter what is known as "No Contact" mode if you detect this behavior while dating her. What is "No Contact"? This is a predetermined time frame during which you do not contact or respond to your girlfriend until she misses you, which could take anywhere between 15 and 30 days, maybe longer. To give you and your girlfriend space to examine your relationship and recover your feelings for one another. She will let you know where you stand if she reaches out. If not, you let her go.

It gives her time to think about you and comprehend what has happened. I understand that for some guys, this is challenging, but if you can master this method, it will spare you a great deal of heartache.

During a no-contact breakup, it is important that you avoid communication of any kind with each other. No texts, no messages on social media, nothing. This may give you and your partner the time to consider everything you need to consider. In addition, it would be a good idea to stay out of her way physically as well. I know this can be difficult if you live in the same neighborhood or work in the same office, but avoiding her in those situations is also difficult.

If you see your girlfriend during this no-contact period, it could lead to an awkward scene. You don't want to be rude or offensive, nor do you want to be coy and defensive. So, if you can't avoid her, smile and nod, and continue on your way. If she wants to break the no-contact rule, that's up to her. Remember that this came about because of her behavior.

Unfortunately, some women enjoy drama; it gives them a sense of pleasure to have their emotions tugged on. I don't think it's a conscious decision, but I can say it can be an issue. For some women, if they don't have their emotional highs and lows in a relationship to keep their interest, they become bored and angry. A few therapists have studied this behavior and called it "trauma bonding," which stems from being in an abusive relationship at some point in the past.

Trauma bonding is the attachment an abused person feels for their abuser, specifically in a relationship with a cyclical pattern of abuse. (Resnick, 2022). Similar to Stockholm syndrome, it frequently happens between the abuser and the abused, and it can make someone leaving an abusive relationship feel overwhelmed and confused.

Older women, in my experience dating, seem to demonstrate this more frequently, perhaps because they have more life experience than younger women.

In Lori Gottlieb's book, *Marry Him: The Case for Settling for Mr. Good Enough*, she discusses the trauma that most women experience as to why they are still single. Lori Gottlieb, a psychotherapist, claims that the way people date today is that women will go on a first date with a guy and will enjoy themselves immensely.

However, when she leaves the date and goes to tell her friends, "the date was a lot of fun, but I still don't feel any butterflies." So, she looks for the next guy to date until she gets that feeling in the pit of her stomach.

As a result, it is impossible to get to know anyone since she is constantly juggling multiple people who are each attempting to make the most of their opportunities on a date. In a recent study, there were women who were asked why they didn't give a guy a second date or were interested in continuing to see the new guy.

According to Dr. Gottlieb, many women answered that "there weren't sparks or butterflies." Sometimes the sparks or butterflies or that feeling of being in love usually come from things like trauma bonds, where the woman might be used to someone being inconsistent or overly aggressive in the relationship, and that becomes the spark she is looking for.

So when she meets a man who's more stable or more consistent and responsive, she doesn't have that excitement or adrenaline rush. She now believes there is no spark in the date. Some women will see this as a red flag and keep dating guys, even though the guy is bad news and things never work out for them when dating other guys.

The reason for this is that many women haven't worked through whatever issues they may have had in previous relationships and will continue to choose men who are similar to what she was used to in previous relationships, even if she believes she is choosing the opposite.

If a relationship is going well and conflicts are few and far between, some women will miss the drama. Because they like the surge of adrenaline and emotional impulses, women occasionally get bored more easily than men.

What should you do if a woman suddenly gets moody for no apparent reason? You must first decide if this is something you can endure and put up with. She won't alter her behavior any time soon. A woman will constantly confront you with some sort of challenge. Considering this, you must determine whether you can live with it. And in order to get through it, you must remain firm. So when a woman is upset, much like in a storm, the feminine is in nature, and a woman's emotions change just like the weather.

The worst thing you can do as a man is to respond to the storm when it comes since that will just lead to conflict and argument. It is a man's duty to be as ineffective as possible while still being a rock of strength when she is feeling vulnerable. Don't let her know she can throw you off balance. You must remain attentive to her while she is distressed. Don't try to fix it, don't try to change it.

It's challenging to maintain emotional control around a moody woman because the moment you get close to her, you stop coming across as the strong, masculine man she is drawn to. In addition, when you lose your masculine frame around her, she has less respect for you. The key is to not allow her to influence you. Don't allow her to disrupt your sense of manliness or your equilibrium as a man. When that occurs, being playful is a wise course of action. For example, a playful tap on the butt or a kiss on the forehead and the words "you're so cute when you're upset" will allow you to playfully approach whatever you do with her. It will make her realize she can't knock you off your pedestal, and she will succumb to your masculinity.

There is always going to be a very good chance that your girlfriend will be rude and irritable toward you at some point in the future. It can be really annoying when you have a girlfriend and she is moody; therefore, you need to know how to handle these situations appropriately.

Women frequently test men, which is why things like this happen. They test the guy to determine his strength. However, if he fails the test, even the first time and only for a minor infraction, she will feel empowered to act even bitchier and moodier the next time. Until she sees you have no control over her, you don't know how to put your foot down, and you don't know how to be a strong man, she will raise her tests and become more and more challenging, and her bitchiness will rise to another level.

Usually, this results in her losing interest in you over time, which forces her to end the relationship. The most significant thing you can do to manage your girlfriend's emotions is to gain her respect.

If she respects and values you as a high-value man, she will be less likely to behave disrespectfully or irritably. A woman who appreciates a man deeply will never act nasty toward him. However, if she doesn't appreciate the guy, she will flack on you, make you jealous, and cause you all kinds of issues. You must, therefore, show her you are not bothered by her antics. Prove to her that you are the man you claim to be.

In the next chapter, I will tell you about the other emotional issues you are going to have to deal with when you get into a relationship with a beautiful woman.

CHAPTER 7

YOU CAN'T FIX HER

IN THE LAST CHAPTER, I told you about mood swings and some likely causes; now we're going to look at dealing with them. First of all, a woman cannot be fixed. You can never fully resolve a woman's problems, no matter how hard you try. I dated a woman for several months, many years ago; she was the best person I ever met. She was gorgeous, sweet, and considerate. I had hoped that it would eventually develop into something significant. I was so enamored with her that I failed to notice the warning signs of her emotional issues.

Her childhood was the root of many of her emotional problems. One of them was her experience with abandonment when she was a young child. She experienced issues with her mother that she was unable to resolve as an adult. I naturally wanted to fix her as a man. I had no idea that what I was doing was causing her to no longer respect me. not knowing that there is nothing you can do to change a woman's emotions.

Sometimes I would experience an emotional roller coaster with her. She would be delighted to be with me one moment, and then furious with me the next. Usually, for something I had said or done. It was a nightmare that left me exhausted emotionally. I sincerely hope that no man would be willing to endure something like that.

Despite how much I cared for her, I had to come to terms with the fact that I couldn't fix or make her happy. This was when I began to comprehend women and how their emotions may vary like the weather as a result of that encounter. After learning so much from that experience, it became very difficult for a woman to emotionally affect me. I discovered that no matter what you do, you cannot make a woman happy or fix her; it is not your responsibility. She must want to be happy on her own. This lesson was hard for me to learn at first.

One of my ex-girlfriends of three years told me I made her miserable before we officially broke up. When she told me, I suggested to her that perhaps she should be with someone else rather than me being angry with her or trying to make her happy. I didn't think it was my responsibility to keep her amused so she could be content all the time. A man can only offer support and his presence if she needs it.

Some women will make these comments to test your character as a man. They use it as a method of screening out would-be suitors, in my opinion. It's awful, I know, but when you're in a relationship with a woman, it's something a man must endure. She has her ups and downs, emotions, and problems, and you are expected to treat her like a woman. If you're going to start dating, you should be prepared for a woman's mood to alter and fluctuate like the weather.

Expect her to fluctuate between happy and sad moods and to periodically withdraw. There are two ways to respond to this behavior from your girlfriend. To begin with, you must disregard her feelings. To be uninterested in or uncaring about something or someone is to be indifferent. You can also respond to her behavior by mirroring her emotions to dissipate her bad energy. No matter how she feels or what she says to you, you must maintain your positivity to diffuse her negative energy.

Most men believe that their role in a relationship is to try to fix the woman they are with. She will change and grow to love him if they only do this one thing. However, these men are merely deceiving themselves. Because until she wants to be fixed, you cannot fix her. She must progress in life and better herself if she wants to better herself.

However, nothing these guys can do will actually help her. Finding a woman you are attracted to and who has fewer concerns and problems is far preferable. In a relationship, you shouldn't have to struggle or put yourself through stressful situations. Both parties should be striving toward making the relationship stronger, and it should be simple to maintain. Your relationship with a woman should improve your quality of life, not make it more challenging.

It will eventually go wrong if you decide to remain with a woman who has a lot of emotional baggage and you seek to fix her. There is a slim possibility that will happen unless she is cooperative and states, "I want to be better and need your help to fix me." So don't make the error of attempting to be her Prince Charming in an effort to win her affection in exchange for attempting to resolve her emotional problems. You would be better off ending the relationship and taking the lessons with you.

When you adopt the idea of "fixing" a woman, you are attempting to convince her that you are a fantastic guy and that the life she is currently leading can be improved by having you as her partner. And if she allows you to help fix her, you are going to demonstrate to her what is possible.

But unknowingly, the woman does not perceive you that way because, at the moment, she is not content with who she is or what is happening in her life. She might be attempting to start over or discovering something that has been lacking in her life, which confuses her. And the guy tries to persuade her or fix her in the hopes of receiving something in return.

This leads many men to think that if she does this and I do that, she will finally view me as I want her to see me. As a result, the man will gradually lose himself, which will ultimately result in him thinking his part in this love story is over. Being her knight in shining armor failed.

So what can a man do? Taking the lead in a relationship does not mean you have to try to fix everything, although this is a natural thing for a man to do. If a woman goes to another woman with a problem, she will get an empathetic response, a sympathetic ear. If that same woman goes to a man with her problem, he will try to fix it, because he thinks that is what she wants. Wrong!

What she actually wants is someone to vent to. Someone who will listen to her issue and, if she requests it, perhaps offer some advice. Some women just want you to listen. This can be difficult to deal with for most men, even though I've been advocating this kind of behavior throughout this book to not be drawn into her emotional mind games and shit-testing.

On the other hand, if the woman is someone you really like, you're willing to put up with her mood swings in order to stay together, and you think she's worth investing your time and emotions in, then this is what you can do.

1. Try to establish the cause of her behavior. If she's not simply mad at you for something you did or didn't do, then findout what is it?
2. Don't jump to conclusions. Does this sound familiar? "Oh, I get it. This is because…" Men will inevitably try to place problems in a box, to compartmentalize them because they are easier to deal with that way.
3. Don't assume you have all the answers because you're the man in the relationship. It is not unmanly to admit you don't know, but it is manly to say you will help her find out.
4. Suggest going along with her for therapy rather than her seeing a therapist on her own. In tests, women in a couples-therapy group developed significantly better behavioral coping strategies than those in a one-on-one therapy group. (The Conversation, 2017)
5. Don't do or say anything that might be construed as gaslighting. By this, I mean saying things like, "I'm sorry you think I did something wrong," or "I did
   that because I love you," or, "You know I wouldn't say that." These phrases only serve to confuse the person you're trying to fix.

There are plenty of other things you could try, but I think that's enough for starters.

In the next chapter, we look at rejection. Yes, when you are playing the dating game, rejection is inevitable, to a point. It's not the rejection that matters, though, it's how you deal with it. This could be the most important chapter for many of you, so read on.

CHAPTER 8

REJECTION

WHEN IT COMES TO WOMEN, there are two different forms of rejection that men experience. The first is in the approach stage. Some men have a hard time approaching women for fear of being rejected. I've seen guys down a full bottle of beer after being turned down by a woman. I even saw a guy be so afraid of approaching a woman he thought was attractive; the very idea of being rejected by her before he even met her stopped him in his tracks. It was as if he had seen a ghost.

The Approach

I have found that the sting of rejection when approaching and trying to talk to a woman easily passes and it is more satisfying if you take a chance to talk to her. The most important thing is that you took the initiative to show her you are a man by expressing your interest in her. This greatly improves a man's character and builds up his manhood. In addition, it shows her and other women around you who may be in the room that you're masculine enough to go for what you want. If you don't try, it's likely you will later regret it.

When you miss an opportunity to talk to a woman, it makes you feel bad and keeps you awake at night thinking about the time you passed on a certain woman you saw two weeks ago.

From my perspective, the humiliation of rejection wears off quickly, but the ache of regret lingers. The *what if?* questions arise when you decline the chance to speak to a woman you're interested in, out of fear of being turned down. With justification, your subconscious mind tries to persuade you that you should have moved sooner. You need to be aware of this: you must shake off the stench of rejection from a woman and move on, and realize it's not personal. She simply isn't into you. The world is full of women, and you haven't even begun to scratch the surface.

If you approach a woman and make an effort to chat with her, whether you succeed or fail, in the next 30 seconds after you leave, she will have forgotten about you even if you've cautiously walked up to her and unintentionally knocked over a chair. She will go back to using her phone or doing whatever she was doing before you made an ass of yourself.

That, my friend, is the length of a woman's attention span for a man she has never met.

She has mentally moved on to what's important to her, despite the fact that you might care and you'll keep it in your mind for a while. Approaching a woman who you embarrassed yourself in front of is trivial in comparison to all the other issues in the world. The last thing you need to worry about is that incident. It's not the end of the world or going to end your life if you get rejected. You'll be alright, and life will go on. You must realize that no risk comes without reward, so it is better to take the chance than to do nothing at all. That's essentially how life goes.

Despite the fact that rejection is extremely difficult to handle, it can occasionally leave you feeling as though there is no hope for the future of your relationships with women—

a feeling that can occasionally arise on a conscious level and give rise to negative thoughts. This enables you to think about rejection in a more sophisticated way. That's what you're doing.

It's not about being negative or positive, but about remaining neutral and saying, "Hey, this happened, and it's true, but I'm not going to let it bother me." Instead, take this fact of being rejected and think to yourself, "What can I do better next time?" Is there anywhere you may have screwed up by saying the wrong thing to her?

Could you have continued the conversation a little more, or maybe you revealed too much about yourself too soon? You didn't allow yourself to be a mystery, and she won't have a chance to wonder about you if you reveal too much too soon. If you want to know why you were rejected by these women, you should reflect on your contact with them. As a result, using this tactic will enable you to improve as a person, which will enable you to interact with and approach women more effectively and, therefore, attract more women.

Each time you are rejected, fail to obtain her phone number, or otherwise fail to advance the conversation, consider what you did well as well as what you can improve on. Thinking critically, you will benefit from this. Even putting it in writing will force you to think about the interaction in a way that will help you advance in your interactions with women.

However, you don't want to overthink things.

For instance, if you review your approach when speaking to a woman and discover that you did nothing incorrectly and that everything appears to have gone as it should have, but your attempt to speak with her was unsuccessful, that's okay.

You can chalk it up to the fact that the interaction was never meant to be, and that has nothing to do with the fact that you are a loser or bad at approaching women.

Recognize that it has nothing to do with you. Simply put, she wasn't the right woman for you, and this is where you can think more realistically and positively. If you do this, your game will greatly benefit. You can think more positively and realistically of yourself. If you employ this strategy, it will improve your ability to approach women.

The Breakup

The second form of rejection a man will go through is a breakup. Rejection can take different forms after a relationship has ended. For many men, this must be the most horrifying experience they've ever had. Some guys have even injured themselves because of this feeling.

You are expected to be the man in the relationship and to handle rejection by being strong. But no matter what you do, don't show her how heartbroken you are by the breakup. Many women will no longer be interested in you once they notice a weakness in your defense. Therefore, you must handle it as best you can without hurting yourself and work through those feelings, so you can let go. By doing this, you demonstrate your strength and increase your value as a man.

My wife and I separated while we were married. We had been together for five years. There were moments when I had trouble falling asleep. And this was back when not everyone had access to social media, cell phones, computers, and all the other means of communication that we now take for granted.

Because of this, I was unable to pursue her and ask her to come back when I wanted to. She was gone once she moved out of our place, and I had no idea where she had gone. While, I continued to have a hard time sleeping at night. It wasn't like I was crying my eyes out, but I was miserable and depressed that I was now alone in my bed. And because I couldn't sleep, I needed something else to do. After I got over the sadness of my separation, which ultimately led to divorce, I started going to the gym almost every day. I pretty much had nothing else to do but get myself in shape and start reading books.

I took all my trauma and heartbreak and focused my energy on becoming a personal trainer and becoming very knowledgeable about the things I wanted in my life, which have helped my career tremendously. Therefore, rejection from a woman can be a great motivator. The reason rejection can be a great motivator is that if you go to a guy these days who is heartbroken and depressed, he will have all the motivation in the world to send 300 text messages to get his girl back instead of using that energy to improve himself and become successful.

To be honest, some of the greatest accomplishments of my life have come after being rejected or heartbroken. The energy you get from being rejected is your revenge if you use it in a positive way. Some guys will get butt hurt about being rejected and wallow in self-pity, but this will make your ex feel justified in dumping you. What a loser you turned out to be.

Whether she dumped you or rejected you, my opinion is that you should use that energy to show that she made a major mistake. Whatever the situation may be, go out and become a millionaire, a musician, or a successful businessman. Then, one day, she's going to look up when she's 40 to 50 pounds heavier in a year's time and regret seeing you do better than when she left you.

Internally, your ego will be like, "You messed up, rejecting me." The key takeaway here is that when it comes to being rejected, life is going to hurt you one day, and how you deal with the pain of rejection is completely up to you. You can either use that pain to galvanize yourself as a man and become the best version of yourself or live a depressed, sad life. No contest.

I Saw It Coming

It's funny how all of your family and friends saw it coming, but you didn't. When my ex walked out on me, it came right out of the blue. Why? I was blind. The signs were there, but I didn't see them. Or maybe I saw them but didn't want to face reality.

So, what are the signs? Well, that depends largely on her reason for leaving. If you've been abusive toward her in some way, then that's up to you, but if you've been good to her, it is hard to take.

These are the things to look out for:

- She is distant, not wanting to be intimate
- She works late
- She goes out more often with friends
- She goes to the gym more often
- She has a new friend she mentions a lot (male or female)

She gets text messages she doesn't like to tell you about.

A lot of the signs are indications of a change in her patterns. It's as though she's preparing for a new life without you. These are not necessarily signs that she's having an affair, although in my experience, women like to have a fresh pair of arms to fall into when they break up with a man.

If you spot any of these signs, you need to wise up. The split may be inevitable, but at least you can be prepared and make sure it happens on your terms.

In the next chapter, we take a look at dating apps. Dating websites have been around for over 20 years, but apps are a relatively new thing and it's important that you understand how these have changed the rules about dating, especially for women.

CHAPTER 9

DATING APPS

IN THE BOOK *Marry Him* by Lori Gottlieb, she claims that a study was conducted on people she refers to as maximists—those who demand nothing less than the best in everything they choose (Gottlieb, 2011). Satisfiers, on the other hand, frequently adopt an attitude of "this is good enough" in interpersonal relationships. They usually have a clear idea of what they want, and when they find someone who meets their strict requirements, they are happy.

For instance, let's say you're looking to buy a new leather jacket. You visit the store and fall in love with a fantastic leather bomber jacket. It fits perfectly and is unlike any other leather jacket you've seen since the one worn by Tom Cruise in the Top Gun movie. The first time you wear it out with the guys, you get lots of compliments, which makes you feel great about your new jacket. This is a satisfier.

A maximist is likely to look at the jacket and decide not to purchase it. They do this because they want to see if they can find something better. Or the maximist might purchase the new jacket, but the following day when they go out on the town with friends, they happen to walk by clothing stores and see another leather jacket in the store window and then they think, "Wow, look at that leather jacket. Maybe I should've bought that one," even though they are receiving compliments on the one they are wearing.

In essence, maximists are never content because they are constantly striving to take their happiness to the next level and achieve what they perceive to be superior, whereas satisfiers are content with what they desire and value.

When using a dating app, people tend to be like that more often than not, especially women. They go on a date but complain that while they had a good time; they didn't feel any butterflies or sparks. But she thinks, "It was great hanging out with him, and I'll definitely see him again."

As she is driving home from her date, she finds all these notifications on the dating app from men who might be interested in her. When she gets home, she scans the list of men who have liked her profile and thinks, "Maybe that guy is better." The issue with this is that these ladies are always juggling multiple guys while attempting to reach their full potential, which prevents them from ever getting to know anyone properly. People should not be treated this way by either women or men, like a throwaway commitment that you simply discard whenever you're bored or run into someone you think might suit you better.

I have seen this more among older women I've dated who didn't want to hurt my feelings. One sent me a text to say, "Although it was wonderful to meet you, there was no spark or connection." This happened right after she got home and came as no surprise because I felt that too—not in me, but in her. I could sense that part of her was looking beyond this date and onto the next one.

When it comes to dating apps, the first piece of advice I can give you is don't let them consume you completely. I am aware that it has become standard practice in recent years to use dating apps to find a partner, but you must realize that women are pros at using dating apps and cellphones. This gives them an advantage in weeding out potential suitors. A dating app makes the ideal filtering system for women to find the person they believe is best for them and the numbers are very much stacked in their favor with most apps.

Compared to TikTok and Instagram, I would rank dating apps as the third best way for a woman to attract as much attention from men as she desires in terms of finding a partner. When using these apps, you should exercise extreme caution because a woman can keep you talking to her for weeks on end without ever wanting to meet up. I advise unmatching these types of women if the dating app interaction lasts more than a week and she doesn't want to meet up for coffee or drinks in person. She's probably just keeping your attention until some other guy she matched with asks her out. Or in case the other guy she's maybe chatting with doesn't work out, so she still has you to confirm her validation.

To this end, she may even suggest talking on the phone before the two of you meet. Even then, she will screen you before meeting you. During the phone call, before she agrees to meet, a woman will analyze every word you say. The questions you should ask her are how long you've been using the app and how many guys she's met up with? If she says two weeks or a month but hasn't met anyone on the app, that's telling you she is screening the guys she matches with by having a phone conversation that leads to nowhere. And it's not cool because she's wasting your time when you could be meeting someone who actually wants to meet you.

When a woman does this, she most likely wants to find a man who will give her the feeling of butterflies when she speaks to him on the phone, which is almost impossible for two reasons. The first reason is that if a man and woman don't meet in person, it's very difficult for that man to establish a connection. A man needs to touch her and display his affection when he says or does something in order to create attraction. How can you recognize a person's social cues if you've never met them?

Secondly, even if she is attractive or frequently dates, a woman tends to get a little lazy by wanting to converse on the phone and expecting to hear something from a guy that will spark her interest before meeting him. Unless she connects with you by actually meeting you, those butterflies won't exist.

Dan Ariely, an MIT behavioral economist and author of the book Predictably Irrational: The Hidden Forces That Shape Our Decisions, studied people's decision-making abilities and discovered that when people wait too long to make a decision, they become confused about what they want at that moment and they lose interest. Ariely says if we don't know what we want, dating can be hard, and online dating can be harder due to the perception that what you are looking for is objective when using online profiles as opposed to meeting someone in person and having a subjective interaction. And the illusion of objectivity is what's not good when it comes to meeting someone new. (Ariely, 2010)

"The less you know about a potential partner before you meet them," according to Ariely, "the better because it increases the opportunity for mystery to develop."

Men who project mystery tend to attract more women because it piques their interest and makes them want to learn more about him. If online daters communicate too much, such as by texting or phone chats that provide information about each other before meeting, it leaves little room for discovery.

And once they meet and see a flaw in the other person, the mystery is gone. As a result, the other person returns home and resumes online dating in search of someone who appears attractive on paper.

When people want to get a lot of information up front, they think it's a good way to not waste time. From what I've experienced, more women do this than men. wanting to chat on the phone or text several weeks prior to meeting up. I'm hoping to get more information, not to waste time.

Ariely claims that it is harder to be interesting when you know too much about someone you have just met. This results in what is known as the "less is more" effect, which states that if you describe yourself in more amiable terms on a dating profile, you'll be more likable. However, if you write, for example, "I like music," the person reading your profile will automatically assume that you like the same kind of music they do. However, if you put on your dating profile what specific music you enjoy, the person will have different interests and find it less attractive.

So, if she recommends talking on the phone prior to meeting up, take it with a grain of salt and don't stay on the phone long. The longer you talk to her on the phone, she will analyze every word you say and assume she knows everything about you without ever having met you. It is almost a certainty that she will try to filter you out as a potential, and the chances of you making it through her filter are slim to none at all.

Therefore, I suggest you try to meet her in person; that's the best course of action. A man's superpower is his ability to manipulate a situation, so meeting in person is essential for this. Only then can he successfully seduce the woman he is attempting to attract.

"The secret to becoming more attractive to the opposite sex? Good conversation"—according to a survey of 2,000 adults released by the Plenty of Fish dating app. The dating site found that nearly nine in ten people (87%) said that they have found someone better looking after a good chat.

ARE DATING APPS A GOOD THING OR A BAD THING?

Using an app has become second nature for most people with a smartphone or tablet, from booking a vacation to ordering takeout. But using an app for dating is something many shy away from, sometimes with good reason.

Whether dating apps are good or bad depends on what you're looking for, and you need to pick an app that delivers what you want. If you want to find a long-term partner or you're just looking to hook up for a one-night stand, just remember this. The woman on the other end is after the same thing.

Everyone has heard of Tinder, right? It was one of the first cellphone apps based on the success of many dating websites on the Internet in the late 90s and early 2000s. Tinder merged with the Match Group, the owners of Match.com, in July 2017 and became one of the biggest dating apps around at that time.

According to Match.com, in 2020, 40% of Americans used online dating apps, and 20% of committed relationships began online. More than double the number of long-term relationships and marriages originated from contacts made online than those meeting casually in bars and clubs. (Match.com, 2022).

Tinder has a reputation for being an app used by people looking for casual sex without relationships (Sales, 2015), and in a study conducted by Texas Tech University in 2017, some interesting statistics came out. More than half of those taking part said they saw a person they knew to be in a relationship on Tinder. (Weiser, et al. 2017). Three-quarters said they knew male friends and over half had female friends who used Tinder despite having a partner.

Some apps are specifically set up for married people or those in a relationship so they can have an affair. These sites offer total anonymity and usually have a high female-to-male ratio. This in itself should tell you what type of person you're likely to meet, so don't sign up if you're looking for someone to share your life with.

So, if you want to increase your chances of finding somebody you can have a meaningful relationship with, you would be better off using something like eHarmony. With over 10 million active users, eHarmony is one of the biggest dating sites in the US (Consumer Rankings, 2023), and with its personality-based matching system, you have a greater chance of meeting someone you might form a relationship with.

To sum up, dating apps are a great way to meet women for whatever kind of relationship you want—casual sex or something more meaningful—but do your research first.

In the next chapter, I run through some of the scenarios I've worked through over the years. I told you at the outset I would give you the benefit of my experience, and this is it.

CHAPTER 10

SCENARIOS FOR DATING

BEFORE I WRAP THIS UP, in this chapter I wanted to share with you several reactions and scenarios I've dealt with over the years from when I first started dating and didn't know much about women or relationships. I figured the advice I'm about to give you will, if not guide you, at least make you aware of some common replies or comments I've had from women, whether you're just starting out or have been dating for a while.

Nobody ever taught me what to expect from a woman when dating or certain statements you will hear from a woman when you're involved with them a lot of the time. If somebody had told me this information before I started dating. I would have been better equipped to manage my relationships and what a woman meant when she made certain comments to me instead of getting butt hurt and taking their comments personally.

I'm not claiming all women are the same, but I can say some comments I've had from various women, depending on the circumstance, have all been the same. (It's humorous yet, true.) Continue dating if you don't think I'm telling the truth. It's as if most women have the same playbook of statements for every situation in order to effortlessly let men down if they lose interest or aren't interested, to begin with.

In my years of dating women and being in relationships, there is one thing I have learned: a lot of what women say shouldn't be taken personally because they are either speaking to you unconsciously (when I say unconsciously, I'm usually speaking emotionally) or she's attempting to avoid hurting you when she says certain things to you that may affect the relationship. Women do not like to get the feeling of being hated, and I believe that a woman's ego is her greatest weakness. Most women find it the worst thing in the world if someone gets the idea of them being a horrible person.

Here are some scenarios I've come across a lot.

She says you don't communicate enough:

If the woman you're dating complains that you don't call her frequently enough, text her frequently enough or give her enough time while you're just starting the relationship, don't rise to it!

When it comes to creating attraction, you want this, especially when the relationship is just getting started. Make arrangements to meet her if she complains; say you don't like texting long messages and you'd rather discuss things in person. If she starts the communication, she will find it more rewarding than if you make the first move and suggest a meeting instead of exchanging texts on a regular basis. For her to see that you like her company and for her to want you more, you must be present.

She says she is not happy:

When a woman claims to be unhappy or depressed, and she questions your happiness, she wants you to justify why you are not feeling the same. How come you can go around laughing and joking with her when she feels so low?

It typically means that she is getting tired of the relationship and that she is not used to the routine that comes with being in a normal, committed relationship. She has gone through the highs and lows of unhealthy relationships with men like the Chads and Tyrones of this world, so she is subconsciously sabotaging the relationship and trying to get you to emotionally edge her out. So that she can experience the same emotional high that she's used to getting from bad boys like the Chad and Tyrone types.

You can only be yourself and if it is in your nature to be happy, then continue to be so. Don't let her push you into making her decision for her. If she's looking for a way out, let her go. She may soon decide things weren't so bad with you when she finds another Chad or Tyrone, or she may not. Either way, you're better off.

She makes a public scene:

In all honesty, I didn't encounter a woman that acted in this manner until I was in college. The girl I was seeing at the time was disappointed that I didn't travel to her state over the summer break from college. I repeatedly apologized for not seeing her and was informed by her best friend that she didn't want to talk to me. I tried to explain to her the reason I wasn't able to come to visit her was that I was working a summer job.

When I finally ran into her at the cafeteria on our college campus as I was finishing up lunch, I got the bright idea to go sit at the table she was at and attempt to talk to her. She gave me a stern look as soon as I sat down next to her before shouting, "LEAVE ME ALONE!" Her outburst shocked and embarrassed me. After that, I don't recall anything, but me removing myself from the situation quickly. Because there were so many people in the college cafeteria, I didn't bother to look around to see who was watching. I hurriedly left the dining hall and headed to my dorm room.

You can imagine how quickly the rumor of the incident spread among college students on campus. Regardless of what happened, I had to attend my classes despite being aware that everyone on the campus was discussing what happened to Chris Finley and how his girlfriend at the time yelled at him in the public cafeteria. For months I was ridiculed. I could see the guys pointing and laughing, the girls giggling behind their hands.

The story circulated around the college campus until a new incident was brought forward that everyone could talk about.

It was an event I will never forget because I had never really been embarrassed in that manner in front of people unless it was something I caused myself, Like the time I tripped because my shoes were untied or fell while lugging Christmas gifts for family members in a mall's icy parking lot (yes all those things happened to me when I was younger).

Let's imagine she starts a scene when you're both out in public, like at dinner, and everything is going well. At the restaurant table, you are comfortable and enjoying your meal and time with her, when she suddenly asks, "Why are you so happy? I'm not happy."

You continue to smile and reply, "Because I enjoy spending time with you, darling."

"You don't seem to care about how I feel," she replies. "I guess it's all about you." She is attempting to draw you into her feelings when she does this and continues to be negative.

This is her being a Prima Donna. She may have something niggling her and she's annoyed that you didn't spot that. She hates that you continue to smile and look happy while she has an issue with something.

Tell her in a calm manner that you won't succumb to this kind of interrogation. If she carries on being negative and things spiral out of control, such as raising her voice in front of people, end the date quickly, throw a few bucks on the table and leave. This will communicate to her you have limitations and that you won't stand for disrespect or embarrassment.

Let's be friends:

Ah, the timeless words of a person you like or have started dating: "Let's just be friends." She could just as easily say she dislikes you and finds you repulsive. Let's be friends is a common phrase used by women to signify a variety of things. One is that she has other options she wants to consider, and she wants to keep you in her back pocket in case those options don't pan out. Having an emotional supporter, a guy who still wants her in the background is good for her ego.

Another explanation for why you might receive the dreaded "Let's be friends" offer is that she doesn't want to break your heart by letting you know she isn't interested and doesn't want you to hate her. Most women want to be liked, and their egos won't allow them to accept the concept that there may be men out there who don't like them. So they make an effort to be friends.

Guys, if a woman says this to you, she is essentially telling you she does not see herself having a sexual relationship with you, regardless of her motivation. My recommendation is to stop being her friend unless you enjoy suffering mental anguish. Being her male orbiter while she dates other guys is a waste of your time. And if she offers you the option to be friends, I would turn down her invitation. Tell her "No, I don't need any new friends," and move on.

The Breakup Comment:

"I think it would be best for both of us if we didn't see each other again."

I can't tell you how many times I've heard this from a female I was dating when she wanted to end our relationship. Typically, when a woman says this, she has met a man who has been catching her attention for a while and wants to clear the decks. It's funny how she thinks it would be best for both of us when she really means it would be best for her.

In general, women will monkey branch. Monkey branching occurs when your girlfriend or the woman you are dating begins to plan to date someone else. They will break up with you if things with the new guy seem to be progressing, and this happens more frequently than you might imagine. Not all women view men as disposable and leap on to the next person, but it happens. Here's another common breakup comment.

"I don't feel we want the same things anymore."

Another line that includes "we" in it. All the best breakup lines have this element of shared responsibility. She won't admit she's met someone else but wants you to think it's because you've changed in some way.

"I'm not ready to settle down," and "I don't see where this is leading" are saying the opposite thing but come from the same issue. She does want to settle down, but not with you.

All of these breakup comments lead back to the same thing —let's be friends.

Bitchy Behavior:

When a woman suddenly displays bitchiness and criticizes everything you say and do, she is deciding whether she wants to keep the relationship going. She is unsure of how to express to you that she needs time to think without offending you up until she gets to the point where she abruptly distances herself from you by creating drama and excuses.

It might not be something you did, and it might just be a masculinity test. When you notice this pattern, my advice is to either tell her, "Let's take some time apart" and mean it, or to implement a 15–30 day no contact rule until she starts to miss you regardless of what comes first. If she reaches out, it lets you know where you stand with her. However, if she doesn't contact you, you know it's best to let her go and move on. Additionally, this gives her time to reflect and consider her true desires and whether she truly wants to be with you.

SUMMARY

Dating and meeting women aren't particularly tough if you practice meeting people outside your comfort zone, even for the opposite sex. And despite what you would imagine when you fantasize about the woman of your dreams, she is not as untouchable as you may think. When my friends would give me excuses for why they weren't approaching the woman they liked, I would say to them, "Look at it this way: these women are just regular human beings, just like you and me. Simply put, the only difference is that they come packaged better than we do. They go to sleep, eat, and go to the bathroom like everyone else."

As a result, remember that gorgeous women are people just like you when you see one and want to ask her out. They are not the miraculous beings that God has given to mankind. You will discover that because they are people like you, they too have issues. You will always put women on a pedestal unless you start getting comfortable being around them.

You have to take a chance while approaching a woman you're interested in. The only way you'll improve is if you do that. It's okay if you mess up or if she rejects you. The sea is swarming with fish. I assure you that the girl you think is the most stunning woman you have ever seen and the one in a million, there is another that is equally attractive. You simply need to step forward and take your shot.

This reminds me of what the ex-UFC fighter turned social media influencer Andrew Tate stated on one of his podcasts about approaching women in public to ask them out on a date. He said, *"A lot of people think other people care about them more than you do."* Let that sink in.

This strikes me as being especially true when approaching and conversing with women you have never met before. The way you think women view you is not how they do. I still treat them equally, regardless of how attractive they are. Many men mistakenly believe that women are these invincible, holy beings. Because they rarely interact with people of the opposite sex, most men have developed the idea that if a woman they are interested in rejects them, it will be the end of the world. I think these men's fear of speaking to gorgeous women stems from their "you're too good for me" mentality. The issue is one of self-esteem, as they struggle to imagine themselves with a beautiful woman.

FINAL WORDS

In conclusion, I can't even begin to tell you how many guys I've met who put women on a pedestal and assume that they don't want to be approached. When it comes to approaching women, you'll hear the same pathetic justification from guys who are afraid of doing so. I've even come close to arguing with guys about cold-approaching women. In this case, their standard response is, "What if she's married or has a boyfriend? What if you ask her for her phone number and she gets angry?"

When guys use the same lame excuse, it irritates me. First off, never assume a woman doesn't want you to ask for her phone number. She will let you know if she is dating someone or married. Secondly, I don't know any woman who would become angry if you asked her for her phone number. If a woman does get angry at you, there's obviously something wrong with her, or she's got problems, so you shouldn't be dating her in the first place. Sadly, so many men in today's society share these views.

Guys, consider it this way. If your dad didn't approach your mom by attempting to talk to her, you probably wouldn't have existed. But you exist because of your dad's decision to take the chance to ask your mom out on a date.

" As of July 13, 2020, there are 97.948 males for every 100 females in the United States. There are 162,826,299 or 162.83 million males and 166,238,618 or 166.24 million females in *the US. The percentage of the female population is 50.52 percent compared to 49.48 percent male population. In the US, there are 3.43 million (or 3,430,615) more females than males. Out of 201 countries and territories, the United States of America comes in at number 85 in terms of the female-tomale ratio.*

"And the gender ratio in Canada in 2021 is 98.58 males per 100 females. There are 18.90 million males and 19.17 million females in Canada. The percentage of the female population is 50.36% compared to 49.64% male population. Canada has 0.4 million more females than males.

"In addition, the gender ratio in the UK in 2021 is 97.75 males per 100 females. There are 33.72 million males and 34.49 million females in the UK. The percentage of the female population is 50.57% compared to 49.43% male population. The UK has 0.77 million more females than males." (Statistics Times. 2021)

There really are plenty more fish in the sea.

So, if you put in the effort and go out there to be the best version of yourself when approaching women, you have a good chance of meeting and discovering a woman who is as attractive as the one you are obsessed with on TV and in the movies.

ABOUT THE AUTHOR

Chris Finley is the author of **Sigma Male Mentality, Man Up and Stand on Your Own,** and **Alpha Male Mentality**. He enjoys helping others live their best lives and pursue their dreams, relationships, and careers.

Do Not Go Yet; One Last Thing To Do

If you enjoyed this book? Then could you leave a review or tell a friend about the book? Or if it has helped you or maybe given you some things to think about. Let me know, I like getting feedback.

REFERENCES

Ariely, Dan. April 27, 2010. *Predictably Irrational: The Hidden Forces That Shape Our Decisions.* Harper Perennial.

Bowlby, John.1997. *Attachment and loss. Volume 1: Attachment.* London: Pimlico.

Bryans, Bruce. March 13, 2013. *What Women Want In A Man: How To Become The Alpha Male Women Respect, Desire, And Want To Submit To.*

Consumer Ranking. 2023. *Best Online Dating Sites,* Consumer-Rankings.com. Accessed January 2023.

Cotec, Isaac, n.d.. HeroRise. *Holding A Masculine Frame: 3 Skills For Awakening Manhood.* https://www.herorise.us/holding-a-masculine-frame-3-skills-forawakening-manhood/

Cotec, Isaac, n.d.. HeroRise, *Negative effects of Hegemonic Masculinity.* https://www.herorise.us/hegemonic-masculinity-definition-and-how-it-affects-us/

Dodgson, Lindsay. Feb 6, 2018, *What Women Want on a First Date* https://www.businessinsider.com/what-women-want-on-a-first-date-2018-2

Donaldson, Mike. October 1993. Theory and Society, Special Issue: Masculinities: *What Is Hegemonic Masculinity?* https://ro.uow.edu.au/artspapers/141

Exploring Your Mind, June 2020. *The Four Principles of Attraction According to H. T. Reis.* https://exploringyourmind.com/the-four-principles-of-attractionaccording-to-h-t-reis/

Exploring Your Mind, 11 April 2016. *How to Beat the Addiction of Seeking Approval* https://exploringyourmind.com/beat-addiction-seeking-approval/

Good Therapy Blog, 2015. *Needy.* PsychPedia. https://www.goodtherapy.org/blog/psychpedia/needy

Gottlieb, Lori. February 1, 2011. *Marry Him: The Case for Settling for Mr. Good Enough.* Dutton. Published by Penguin Group USA.

Healthline. December 5, 2019. *What Causes Extreme Mood Shifts in Women?* https://www.healthline.com/health/mood-swings-in-women#causes

Hill, Catey. July 18, 2017. Market Watch. *Doing this will immediately make you more attractive to a potential lover.* https://www.marketwatch.com/story/doingthis-will-immediately-make-you-more-attractive-to-a-potential-lover-2017-0718-888435

Kaufman, M. 1999. *Men, feminism and the contradictory experiences of power among men,* originally published in Theorizing Masculinities, Sage Publications, 1994. https://www.michaelkaufman.com/wp-content/uploads/2009/01/men_feminism.pdf

Laderer, Ashley. Nov 29, 2022. *Gaslighting was named word of the year 2022 — here's what it means and 16 things that gaslighters say to manipulate you.* https://www.

    insider.com/guides/health/sex-relationships/gaslighting-examples

Lambert Couples Therapy, 2022. *Familiarity Breeds Contempt.* https://www.

    lambertcouplestherapy.com/familiarity-breeds-contempt/

McLeod, Saul. August 18, 2022. Simply Psychology. *What Is Attachment Theory?*

The Importance of Early Emotional Bonds. https://www.simplypsychology.org/attachment.html

Plenty of Fish dating app blog. https://blog.pof.com/

Reis, H. T., Maniaci, M. R., Caprariello, P. A., Eastwick, P. W., & Finkel, E. J.. 2011. *Familiarity does indeed promote attraction in live interaction.* Journal of Personality and Social Psychology, 101(3), 557–570. https://doi.org/10.1037/a0022885

Resnick, Ariane. November 23, 2022. *What Is Trauma Bonding?* https://www.verywellmind.com/trauma-bonding-5207136

Sales, Nancy Jo, August 6, 2015. *Tinder and the Dawn of the 'Dating Apocalypse'.* Vanity Fair. Retrieved October 29, 2018.

Stacey Laura Lloyd; Sept. 23, 2022. Brides. *How to Stop Being Needy in a Relationship; Plus, why it's important to understand the difference between being needy and clingy.* https://www.brides.com/how-not-to-be-clingy-4176696

Statistics Times. 2021. Demographics: *World-Sex-Ratio* https://statisticstimes.com

Swartz, Karen Lee, n.d. Johns Hopkins Medicine: *Recognizing and Getting Help for Mood Disorders.* https://www.hopkinsmedicine.org/health/wellness-andprevention/recognizing-and-getting-help-for-mood-disorders

The Conversation. May 1, 2017. *Men can help women deal with their PMS* https://theconversation.com/men-can-help-women-deal-with-their-pms-76401

Weiser, Dana A.; Niehuis, Sylvia; Flora, Jeanne; Punyanunt-Carter, Narissra M.; Arias, Vladimir S.; Baird, R. Hannah. 2017. *Swiping right: Sociosexuality, intentions to engage in infidelity, and infidelity experiences on Tinder.* Science Direct. Personality and Individual Differences, Volume 133, 2018, Pages 29-33. https://www.sciencedirect.com/science/article/abs/pii/ S0191886917306311#!

YouGov PLC, 2016. YouGov Survey Results. *The perception of masculinity amongst young men.* https://d25d2506sfb94s.cloudfront.net/cumulus_uploads/document/n8w76t4o98/InternalResults_160511_Masculinity-Femininity_W.pdf

Milton Keynes UK
Ingram Content Group UK Ltd.
UKHW011036201123
432908UK00005BA/711